The Butcher's Apron

The Butcher's Apron

*A dream play comedy
in two acts for six players*

Charles Tidler

Ekstasis Editions

An Inconnu Dramabook

Library and Archives Canada Cataloguing in Publication

Tidler, Charles
    The butcher's apron / Charles Tidler.

A play.
ISBN 1-894800-88-5

    1. Strindberg, August, 1849-1912--Drama. 2. Munch, Edvard,
1863-1944--Drama. I. Title.

PS8589.I34B88 2006   C812'.54   C2006-905461-4

Published in 2006 by:
Ekstasis Editions Canada Ltd.   Ekstasis Editions
Box 8474, Main Postal Outlet   Box 571
Victoria, B.C. V8W 3S1   Banff, Alberta ToL oCo

Ekstasis Editions wishes to thank the following for their support of its publishing program: the Canada Council for the Arts, and the Province of British Columbia through the British Columbia Arts Council.

Playwright's Note

The Butcher's Apron is an expressionistic collaboration based upon the lives and writings of the principle figures of the play, notably August Stringberg, Frida Uhl, Stanislaw Przybyszewski, Edvard Munch and Dagny Juell. Finally, however, it is a work of the imagination written for live theatre and not historical biography.

All printing and performing rights of this play are strictly reserved and in all countries permission to perform it or give readings whether by amateurs or professionals must be obtained in advance from the author: c/o The Belfry Theatre, 1291 Gladstone Avenue, Victoria, B.C., V8T 1G5, Canada.

I wish to thank the following for assistance, support and sympathy: The Banff Playwrights Colony, The Belfry Theatre, The Canada Council, The University of Victoria, CBC Radio Drama, and The New Play Centre.

Act One, Scene Two, was originally published in *Prism international*, Winter 1992.

This play is dedicated in memory of my mother.

—Charles Tidler
August, 2006

The Butcher's Apron was originally produced as a one-hour radio drama for Sextet on CBC in 1988. It was directed and produced in Vancouver, British Columbia, by John Juliani, and starred Morris Panych as August Strindberg.

As a full-length stage play, *The Butcher's Apron* had its world premiere at Theatre Passe Muraille, Toronto, Ontario, on March 16, 1990, with the following cast:

AUGUST/STRINDBERG	Stephen Ouimette
FRIDA UHL	Paulina Gillis
MAN/OTTO/LUDWIG/FIGURE	Bruce McFee
WOMAN/MITZI/WRAITH/DAGNY	Ellen-Ray Hennessy
STACHU	Steven Yorke
EDVARD	Julian Richings

Directed by Brian Richmond.
Set and Costume Design by H.Y. Fung.
Lighting Design by Richard Moffatt.
Soundscape by Don Horsburgh.
Dramaturge — Brian Richmond.
Stage manager — Nancy Dryden.

The Butcher's Apron

"I fought out a terrible battle with the enemy, my own self."
—August Strindberg, *Inferno*

Time:
Three days in April, 1893.

Place:
Berlin.

Characters:
(in order of appearance)
WOMAN.
MAN.
STRINDBERG, 44.
FRIDA, 21.
AUGUST, 44.
OTTO, 55.
MITZI, 30.
STACHU, 24.
EDVARD, 30.
WRAITH.
DAGNY, 27.
LUDWIG.
FIGURE.

The play requires six actors: four men, two women.
One actor plays both AUGUST and STRINDBERG.
One actor plays MAN, OTTO, LUDWIG, and FIGURE.
One actor plays WOMAN, MITZI, WRAITH, and DAGNY.
STACHU must be able to play piano.

The Set:

A bright, open space adaptable to many locations. A pit. A high place. A middle ground. Something oppressive and inhuman upstage, machinery, et cetera. Lots of red sky for Act Two. Minimal props and furniture. Two or three heavy doors. Mirrors. Curtains.

Act One

Scene One. The Black Pig.

(Lights up. A MAN and a WOMAN sit at a table and two chairs. There is a litre of absinthe, glasses, an ashtray. The MAN is drinking and smoking. The WOMAN is writing with a pencil into a small notebook. She pays no attention to the MAN.)

MAN: I was in a restaurant today. Down by the railroad station, a little restaurant, and I was watching a man and a woman eating sausages and gravy... thick, dark chocolate-colored gravy you only find in Berlin, and greasy sausages. At a table opposite, there was another man, and he evidently was the husband of the woman who was sitting with the man eating sausages and gravy because... this was wonderful, a pure moment... the man at the other table got up and walked over and picked up the plate of sausages and gravy, and he threw them in the woman's face. (Short pause.) Isn't that wonderful? Isn't that life? The sausages and gravy dripped all over her head and her hair and all down her dress... chocolate-colored shit all over her face.

(Pause.)

And do you know what happened next? (Short pause.) The first man, the lover... I guess he was the lover of the chocolate-colored woman... he got up from the table and ran away. Out the door. Down the street. And the woman... she got down on her hands and knees and crawled across the filthy floor of the restaurant to the feet of her husband and begged his forgiveness.

(Pause.)

A moment, a pure, wonderful moment.

(Pause.)

How would you like that? (Short pause.) How would you?

11

(Pause.)

I'd like to see you fool around then.

(Pause.)

From this day forward, when I say drink, you will drink.

(Pause.)

Did you hear me? And when I say eat, from this day forward, you will eat. (Short pause.) That's the way it is... today... and forever. Drink... and you drink. Eat... and you eat. And when I say...

(Indicates his crotch.)

You jump on it. Jump on it, and like it. Today. Forever.

(Pause.)

Did you hear me? (Short pause.) Did you...

(Bangs his fist on the table.)

Did you hear me?

(The WOMAN continues to write. The MAN has a riding crop.)

Alright, you asked for it.

(The MAN approaches the WOMAN. She has a small mirror and flashes it into his face. The MAN drops the riding crop.)

You ugly cow.

(Flash. The MAN chokes himself. He lunges at the WOMAN. Another flash, and the MAN repeatedly bangs his head on the table, then goes down in a heap on the floor. He writhes in pain. The WOMAN gathers up her notebook and pencil, then casually exits. The MAN slowly crawls toward a second table where another man has been passed out over a bottle throughout the scene. This man is STRINDBERG. A spotlight picks him up, and he awakes.)

STRINDBERG: Ahh…

(STRINDBERG sees the MAN and is frightened.)

Are you my shadow?

(STRINDBERG grabs and shakes the MAN.)

Are you my shadow?

MAN: What is the meaning— Let go of me—

STRINDBERG: Where am I? Is this Hell?

MAN: Take your hands off—

STRINDBERG: Where am I?

MAN: This is the Black Pig, you idiot. You're drunk—

STRINDBERG: A tavern?

MAN: Yes. Let go—

STRINDBERG: Which city, which century, which year— Tell me. Speak.

MAN: This is Berlin, April, 1893.

STRINDBERG: Berlin? Of course, he would come to Berlin.

MAN: What do you want— Money?

STRINDBERG: I am August Strindberg… the real Strindberg. I'm the victim of a doppelganger, double-goer, double-walker. He's stolen my heart, cut it right out of my body.

MAN: You're mad.

STRINDBERG: I was left for dead in a boxcar full of cattle en route to the slaughterhouse. A superman in a boxcar—

(The MAN breaks free and runs away.)

MAN: Police! Police! Soldiers—

(He exits.)

STRINDBERG: I have seen the ovens. I have wrestled with the butcher.

(STRINDBERG opens his shirt and bares his chest. There is no wound, no scar, nothing amiss. End of scene.)

Scene Two. The Library.

(A door. A small desk and chair. A divan. A bookshelf. A telephone. FRIDA sits at the desk. She wears an expensive and provocative evening gown and is talking on the telephone. Somewhere, in another room, a cello is being played.)

FRIDA: (on the phone) Hello, dearest Sister… it's Frida. I'm calling from the library. The reception—

(Pause.)

I know it's late, past midnight, but… guess what? August Strindberg is here. (Short pause.) Strindberg, the great misogynist, playwright, genius. He's here, tonight, in this house, dressed like the Flying Dutchman. I have an interview with him for the morning paper. I'm going to nail the Nordic pretender to the wall. (Short pause. Laughs.) I have my ways.

(Pause.)

I'm not going home with you to Vienna. I thought we settled that. It took me twenty-one years to escape my father's house— (Short pause.) Munich? No!

(Pause.)

I told you, I love Berlin. My daily life is a sweet volatile mix of the bohemian and the bourgeois. I starve for days at a time and in between drink champagne. My education is suffering a complete breakdown. The artists and writers among whom I circulate are the most unnatural, unwholesome, eccentric, queer, odd... nothing but talent.

(Pause.)

Sister, I am a journalist and a critic.

(AUGUST, dressed in tux and tie and a great flowing cape, suddenly appears at the library door. He carries large green linen bag fastened at the top by a large black button. He winks at FRIDA, and she winks back.)

Here he is. (Short pause.) Strindberg. I'll see you back at the apartment. (Short pause.) I don't know when... sister, goodbye.

(Hangs up.)

STRINDBERG: It was hard work shaking them off, but here I am.

VOICE: (offstage) Strindberg... Strindberg...

FRIDA: Quick. We can close the door.

(AUGUST enters the library. FRIDA closes the door. She has a key.)

AUGUST: (laughing) Those old fakers, farts... patrons of the arts, indeed.

(Meanwhile, FRIDA locks the door.)

FRIDA: No one shall disturb us.

AUGUST: (going on, mocking the outside world) If science interferes with progress, science must reverse itself.

(FRIDA hides the key. A knock at the door.)

FRIDA: Shh!

VOICE: (behind the locked door) Hello. Who's there?

(Another knock.)

Strindberg...?

(A long pause. FRIDA listens at the door.)

FRIDA: He's gone.

AUGUST: Oh, thank god for that.

(They laugh together.)

Receptions, my young lady, oh how I hate them. Theatre managers, actors, playwrights... always trying to borrow money, or to steal an idea.

(Shudders.)

Sometimes I get a raging desire to say exactly what's on my mind, but if people were really frank and honest, the world would collapse.

FRIDA: Boom! Let it.

AUGUST: Ah, a library. We're among friends here.

FRIDA: Yes... we are.

AUGUST: Indeed, mademoiselle.

FRIDA: Duck, duck, goose?

AUGUST: Duck...?

FRIDA: It's a game. Don't you know it?

AUGUST: Yes, of course I do.

FRIDA: Well, then... duck, duck, duck... goose.

AUGUST: I'm the goose?

(FRIDA nods.)

Well, you are a young lady and have to be careful about your... reputation.

FRIDA: I want to write books, and you are August Strindberg.

AUGUST: That is exactly what you will never be forgiven. But I have never yet caused gossip about any nice girl.

FRIDA: Only the not-so-nice ones cause gossip?

AUGUST: Well, aren't we clever.

FRIDA: I have read all of your plays... the novels, too.

AUGUST: (amused) You have? All of them? Are you sure?

FRIDA: I have devoured you.

AUGUST: (alarmed) Devoured me?

FRIDA: Like a hungry beast.

AUGUST: Who are you?

FRIDA: Who am I, Herr Strindberg?

AUGUST: Yes.

FRIDA: I am Frida Uhl... but we have already been introduced.

AUGUST: Frida Uhl... (Short pause.) And where do you come from, Frida Uhl? What is the story of your life? You see, you remind me of someone I once knew... centuries ago it now seems, and you may be... (Short pause.) Have you ever seen your mother dead in a box?

FRIDA: My mother is very well, thank you.

AUGUST: Do you believe in reincarnation?

FRIDA: I believe in reclamation, equality, and the battle of the brains.

AUGUST: What is the first thing you remember?

FRIDA: My father's voice: Obey!

AUGUST: Do you remember the womb?

FRIDA: (laughs) No.

AUGUST: I do... the womb-of-the-dead-twin.

FRIDA: Dead twin...?

(A spotlight comes up on STRINDBERG.)

STRINDBERG: Ever since I was born, I have always had a rival, a ghostly twin who got everything while I got nothing. From the very beginning, my mother nursed my shadow in the warm, bright kitchen while I was left alone in the damp nursery with the door closed. Like a potato in a cellar, my hungry howls sprouted in the darkness, bellowing for one drop of sweet human kindness. Mercy. (Short pause.) Oh, what a rotten rat shit inferno I've had to put up with all my life. All my life. My twin brother. The ugly sucking vampire.

(Pause.)

One day my shadow brother brought into the house a dead ladybug, and mother, who was always so busy with pots and pans and pietism, somehow found the leisure time to construct a miniature casket of cedar wood, and she and my vampire brother buried the ladybug behind the rhubarb in the garden. A ladybug. You could pinch it between your fingers. (Short pause.) I learned the Latin names and the precise habits of each and every thoracic insect within the city limits of Stockholm... and mother smacked me across the face for muddying my galoshes in pursuit of the last elusive species. (Short pause.) My brother, my rival, scrawled a stick-figure caricature of the king of Sweden. Mother baked him a pudding. At the age of six, I mastered the art of painting in watercolors. My sense of perspective was astounding. All my efforts, into the garbage. (Short pause.) My shadow, my twin, had two lines, two lines, in a Christmas pageant, and mother made him a white linen shirt with mother-of-pearl buttons. I composed a thousand-line epic poem celebrating the compassion of Christ. Mother lectured me on the sin of pride: Seek ye to be forever simple-minded.

(Pause.)

My mother was pale and sickly, transparent like a pelargonium. Do you know that flower, forever foreign to the goodness of the sun, consumptive white leafs shot with blood...?

(The spotlight fades.)

AUGUST: A digression. Please... tell the truth, what is the first thing that you remember?

FRIDA: The first, the very first thing I can remember... well, yes, it was the sun. The laughing sun. And for years, even now, if the sun smiles on me, I am happy... very, very, very happy.

AUGUST: What month were you born?

FRIDA: I was born in April... in Austria.

AUGUST: Sun on snow, then.

FRIDA: Yes.

AUGUST: Blinding purity. The Madonna. Of course, it is you, isn't it?

(Pause.)

FRIDA: The second thing I remember is not so pleasant.

AUGUST: I know.

FRIDA: You do?

AUGUST: You are an orphan.

FRIDA: No.

AUGUST: No? Are you sure?

FRIDA: Quite sure I'm not an orphan... but something of a gypsy, I suppose.

AUGUST: You see, I know. Please... a little exposition.

FRIDA: I... (Short pause.) How do I say this? I... I did not come into the world because my father loved my mother, but because he loved another woman he was trying to forget.

AUGUST: You poor child. God bless you.

FRIDA: As a... remedy? Yes, that's the word. As a remedy to my parents' marriage, I was a failure I'm sorry to say. They, my mother and father, soon separated after my birth. Mother returned to her family's estate on the Danube... very, very rich, very, very dull. (Short pause.) Father moved to Vienna. He's the editor-in-chief of the Imperial Gazette, Austria's largest and most powerful newspaper. (Short pause.) My parents put me in one convent school after another. London, Paris, Italy, Switzerland, everywhere the bright sun shines, but especially Paris, which I love like a sister. (Short pause.) I hate... hated all the schools, the pious hypocrisy, the superficial education. (Laughs.) Ten years of virginal incense among the brides of God. But to live in a new country each new year was wonderful. Wanderlust inflamed my blood, the hot sun, and I have become... what? A sophisticated, pantheistic sensualist, I suppose. (Laughs.) 'You don't live, you vegetate,' says my father. (Short pause.) And now, I love Berlin. I do. Always so much noise and shouting. It resembles a gold-mining town in America... don't you think so?

AUGUST: Well… a young emperor is building himself a capitol.

FRIDA: Life beats high, and the sun, the sun shines on Berlin.

AUGUST: Ignis fatuus… even in the middle of the night.

> (Pause.)

FRIDA: Herr Strindberg, what are you doing?

AUGUST: Circumnavigating your navel with my index finger.

FRIDA: Oh…

AUGUST: Is that not an accurate description?

FRIDA: Please… stop.

AUGUST: Who are you? Really, I mean. Tell me.

FRIDA: I don't know what you mean.

AUGUST: One last time, what is your real name?

FRIDA: I told you, I am Frida Uhl.

AUGUST: Frida Uhl…

FRIDA: Herr Strindberg, please…

AUGUST: I beg, call me August.

FRIDA: August, stop it.

> (Pause.)

AUGUST: So then, now I know. You are the cruel Madonna who sharpens her teeth… who boils to a thin, rancid soup the hundred bones of her children.

FRIDA: I have no children.

AUGUST: You stand exposed.

FRIDA: I don't know what you're talking about.

AUGUST: You don't?

FRIDA: No, I don't.

AUGUST: Do you… want to fuck me? (Short pause.) Well?

FRIDA: As a lady, I'll pretend I didn't hear—

AUGUST: You're no lady. You're a woman. A woman who locks the library doors. Yes, I saw you. You think you're precious? Priceless? Fragile? Unique? Intellectual? Super-modern? Liberated? The Stronger? Which? How many? All? The living feminine contradiction? Ha. You must know, I left behind two dozen of your like in Sweden. Give me a fortnight, and I shall do at least as well in Berlin. Well, bring out the sabres… the pistols. What's your retort?

FRIDA: My retort is this: I am both serious and professional, Herr Strindberg.

(FRIDA goes to the desk.)

Ink. Pen. Paper. Shall we interview?

AUGUST: Have you read Nietzsche?

FRIDA: Yes.

AUGUST: And?

FRIDA: I, too, expect and hope for something new to come into the world.

AUGUST: You are a feminist. Or think you are.

FRIDA: Because I express sentiments that differentiate me from a doormat? (Short pause.) We live in exciting times, Herr Strindberg.

AUGUST: August.

FRIDA: Today, a twenty-one year old female seizes the will to power.

AUGUST: Oh...?

FRIDA: You think that because of my father... to be sure, I begged and plotted to win my position as a Berlin theatre correspondent, but it is by my merits alone my by-line continues to appear.

AUGUST: Congratulations.

FRIDA: Shall we interview?

AUGUST: No.

FRIDA: Yes, we must. I insist.

AUGUST: On the battle of the brains? No. Not until I know who you are. Who you really are. You remind me of someone I once knew a long time ago. I am trying to trace, but my memory is a complete blank. (Short pause.) You want to write books?

FRIDA: Yes.

AUGUST: Then you must learn something about writing. There's no profession so crude, so devoid... if you knew what life looks like after... after you, the writer... after...

FRIDA: There is great beauty to be found in the treasures of literature.

AUGUST: Flowers are beautiful... not words.

FRIDA: As a writer, you have no faith in the world.

AUGUST: Faith in the games that children play.

FRIDA: Does anything fulfill its promise?

AUGUST: Only the imagination.

FRIDA: Shall we... shall we interview?

AUGUST: Yes, let's.

FRIDA: Good.

>   (Pause.)

The great poet, playwright, novelist—

AUGUST: Chemist.

FRIDA: You, Herr August Strindberg, have recently been divorced in Sweden. The echo of your divorce has resounded throughout Berlin like a battle cry.

AUGUST: Yes... placed between two alternatives, either to kill a woman or to be killed by her, I took a third one. I, I... left her.

FRIDA: And...?

>   (Pause.)

And... Herr Strindberg?

AUGUST: Yes... yes, excuse me. What was the question?

FRIDA: Your divorce—

AUGUST: That word! It's like an axe. I can scarcely speak... breathe...

>   (Pause.)

FRIDA: Another tack, perhaps?

AUGUST: Yes, please...

FRIDA: Today, in Berlin, one reads only French and Scandinavian books. The young German writers, since the seventies, have got all their ideas from the North. There true genius lies.

AUGUST: Well… I am forty-four, an exile, and an orphan, with only a trunk for my servant. And the spring of 1893 finds me in Berlin, living as a bachelor in a furnished room—

(A spotlight picks up STRINDBERG.)

STRINDBERG: Living as a superman in a boxcar.

(The spot dies.)

FRIDA: Did you say… 'boxcar'?

AUGUST: Boxcar…?

FRIDA: Yes. Did you say you are living in a boxcar?

AUGUST: I said… I am living as a bachelor in a furnished room.

(Pause.)

FRIDA: You have a reputation as being the great woman-hater. Is that correct?

AUGUST: I am always asked this question. The woman-lover would be closer to the truth.

FRIDA: Yet in your book, A Madman's Defense—

AUGUST: Here we go.

FRIDA: In which you vivisect your wife like a trussed frog—

AUGUST: I can scarcely breathe outside the presence of a woman.

FRIDA: Is it not true what you said?

AUGUST: What… that I was married to a cow wench, a phonograph, a vampire? Absolutely.

FRIDA: How can you speak so about the woman who has been your wife?

AUGUST: I see—

FRIDA: No woman, in the history of the world, ever said or did what you attribute to her.

AUGUST: I see my ex-wife has already her congregation in Berlin. She's the holy martyr in the church of the third sex. I shall have to rewrite the whole of theology, criminology, economic theory, and at least add a whole new chapter to botany merely to be understood.

FRIDA: Define the third sex.

AUGUST: The manly-woman, of course, who wears pants and smokes cigars, spawning a whole generation of lacy, lily, paper-dolly men.

FRIDA: Your logic astounds me. Have you any evidence?

(AUGUST unbuttons the linen bag and pulls out a whip.)

AUGUST: The man brings the whip to the woman who sharpens her teeth.

(AUGUST snaps the whip.)

FRIDA: You have a whip, but you have no evidence.

AUGUST: Ask yourself, can one love and not hate?

(Snaps his whip.)

FRIDA: Put that silly thing away.

AUGUST: We are all so much entangled, man and woman… things can't be put right but must be burned up, blasted, butchered.

(The whip hangs at his side.)

FRIDA: Then do it. Clear the boards. A new race, the superman and the feminist, will create a new world.

AUGUST: Ugh, impossible.

>   (AUGUST drops the whip, sinks down upon the divan, and
>   hides his face in his hands.)

FRIDA: But they must, they must. The status quo, man's domination of
woman, is a monster.

>   (Pause.)

Herr Strindberg…?

>   (Pause.)

You must understand, it is not always easy to be charming when one is
mad with rage. Hardly a night goes by in Berlin but a woman is brutally
murdered.

>   (Pause.)

Herr Strindberg.

>   (A spotlight picks up STRINDBERG on the divan. He looks up.)

STRINGBERG: I am August Strindberg, the real August Strindberg. I'm the victim of a doppelganger. A shadow, a double-goer walks in my shoes, talks
through my mouth. Thief! Criminal!

>   (STRINDBERG produces a dagger and stabs the air behind his
>   back, never at FRIDA.)

Where is he? Where? Where?

FRIDA: Herr Strindberg—

STRINDBERG: Where is he? Where? There? Here?

FRIDA: Please, put the dagger away—

STRINDBERG: Where? There—

FRIDA: You don't have to fight in here. Please—

STRINDBERG: What, this isn't the earth?

FRIDA: It's the library.

STRINDBERG: This is earth. You're not fooling me. Earth… where they mate and destroy.

(Stabs the air.)

As long as the mechanism keeps running, it's kick and scratch and fight with your hands and feet for all you're worth.

(Fighting the air.)

Where? There. Here—

FRIDA: No, no… please… please—

STRINDBERG: Outside the courtroom following my divorce, my wife of thirteen years, my ex-wife, came up to me and said, 'Well, did you get what you wanted?' And I said, 'When the time comes for me to die, I'll be able to say I don't owe anybody anything, and I never got anything for nothing.'

(Stabs the air.)

'Everything I own, I had to fight for.'

(STRINDBERG puts the dagger to his throat.)

Here he is. I've got him by the throat—

FRIDA: Herr Strindberg, no!

STRINDBERG: Who are you? Who are you?

FRIDA: Don't be afraid.

STRINDBERG: A woman— Ahh…!

(STRINDBERG drops the dagger, moves behind the divan.)

Don't touch me! Don't—

(STRINDBERG flees. The sound of a regiment of soldiers marches through the library.)

Berlin. The air snaps with the will to power, and the earth is a paved parade ground for marching toy soldiers. Blood and iron. The survival of the fittest. The battle of the sexes. The revolution of the elite. Drums. Guns. March march march march march…

(The soldiers fade into the distance.)

Beware the shattered day when soldiers fight wars in the sky, and Berlin is a raging curtain of flesh and fire.

(Pause.)

I am August Strindberg. I move in and out of worlds, step in and out of roles. I range freely across time. I am the dreamer, the artist, the superman. I know the past and the future. But look, look here.

(Pause.)

I have no heart, no heartbeat, no present. I am completely isolated from the momentary world of man, woman, and child.

(Pause.)

FRIDA: Herr Strindberg…? Are you… can I… would you like something?

STRINDBERG: Life is hard… like when you pull a hook out of a fish's throat, and the heart follows.

(The spotlight fades.)

AUGUST: Oh, hello… mademoiselle.

FRIDA: Hello…

AUGUST: Now, what was the question?

FRIDA: Question…? (Laughs.) I've… forgotten. Are you alright?

AUGUST: Wasn't it something about the feminist and the superman creating a new world?

FRIDA: Yes, it was, but you—

AUGUST: What do you think?

FRIDA: What do I think?

AUGUST: Yes.

FRIDA: Are you… please, Herr Strindberg, don't patronize me.

AUGUST: I never would. (Short pause.) Do you believe, for example… this new world will retain the institution of marriage?

FRIDA: A new, modern marriage, yes.

AUGUST: How so?

FRIDA: Marriage must become a free contract between equals… but on the liberation of women—

(AUGUST discovers the dagger on the floor.)

AUGUST: Oh… has someone been here looking for me? Well?

FRIDA: What do you mean, someone looking for you?

AUGUST: While I was away, someone has been here.

(AUGUST picks up the dagger and puts it in the bag.)

FRIDA: While you were away?

AUGUST: I have the power... my soul has the ability to escape my body.

FRIDA: Is that easy to do?

AUGUST: Not difficult really, not for me, but it is tiring. Sometimes I remember every detail and could write a story.

FRIDA: Where does your soul go?

AUGUST: Well, sometimes, I go for a walk on the beach beyond the stars.

FRIDA: You mean your Swedish islands.

AUGUST: (laughing) No, no, dear girl, Sweden, the last time I looked anyway, is still to be found on the planet Earth.

FRIDA: You walk in the sky.

AUGUST: Yes. And I have discovered that the stars are peepholes.

FRIDA: Peepholes, Herr Strindberg?

AUGUST: Absolutely. If you walk up close enough to the stars, you can look through them and see Paradise on the other side, blazing with glory. You can. You see, I believe in transmutation. All knowledge can be reduced to one element.

FRIDA: You believe in alchemy.

AUGUST: I believe in a primary matter out of which all the elements have developed by splitting, condensation, dilution, copulation, crossing, et cetera, et cetera.

FRIDA: You are saying you can make gold.

AUGUST: Aha...

(AUGUST digs into the bag.)

I could... evade... a direct answer to your skepticism by saying... oh, something like... the fact that I can trace the evolution of the common housecat, felinus domesticus, does not mean I can hocus pocus produce a wildcat out of the bottom of my hat. But I need no evasion. Here is my reply.

(AUGUST produces a couple strips of scorched yellow gauze permeated with tiny golden specks.)

Behold.

(Gives the strips to FRIDA. Pause.)

Well...?

FRIDA: Is this gold?

AUGUST: More or less a finished gold.

FRIDA: What do you mean by more or less?

AUGUST: An intermediary stage between common sulfur and pure gold. If I were to properly remelt it with copper and some other substances, et cetera, et cetera, the result might be a refined gold.

FRIDA: Then, so far, it is not gold after all—

AUGUST: It is!

FRIDA: Then one could use these products, Herr Strindberg, to increase one's cash funds?

AUGUST: What? Sell science for money? What a sin. Disgusting.

(AUGUST takes back the strips.)

Thank you.

(Puts them away in the bag. A hard knocking is heard from the other side of the locked door.)

VOICE: Hello… hello… anybody there?

FRIDA: (whispers) It's Otto. Shall we unlock the door?

AUGUST: Yes. Let's not have scandal.

FRIDA: I've misplaced the key.

AUGUST: Find it at once!

OTTO: (knocking) Hello… who's there?

AUGUST: The key! The key!

FRIDA: I can't find it.

(AUGUST throws himself at the door and tries to open it by brute force to no avail.)

OTTO: (knocking) Hello… unlock the door.

AUGUST: That's what we're trying to do.

FRIDA: Aha!

AUGUST: You've got it?

FRIDA: No. It's disappeared.

AUGUST: Torture me in hell.

FRIDA: Otto, please stop pounding on the door.

OTTO: Well, you two: The wild Swedish Lion and the youngest woman in literary Berlin… locked away in the library.

FRIDA: I've misplaced the key.

AUGUST: I didn't know it was locked.

(OTTO is laughing.)

I assure you, Herr Neumann-Hofer—

FRIDA: Otto! Stop laughing.

(OTTO controls himself.)

I am interviewing Herr Strindberg for my newspaper column, and I have every intention of concluding my interview with Herr Strindberg. Then we shall commence a thorough search of the library for the key. Am I understood?

OTTO: (chuckles) Of course, conclude the interview. I'll wait for you in the drawing room.

FRIDA: Herr Strindberg has graciously offered to see me home to my apartment.

AUGUST: I have?

OTTO: (chuckles) Strindberg knows best.

FRIDA: Good night, Otto.

(Pause. AUGUST listens at the door.)

AUGUST: Well, I guess he's gone.

FRIDA: Look.

(FRIDA has the key.)

AUGUST: You had it all along?

FRIDA: Yes.

AUGUST: Well, well, let's conclude the interview.

FRIDA: Let's.

>(Pause.)

>Herr Strindberg... what is your final observation on the institution of marriage?

AUGUST: As constituted today, it's like watching animals being butchered.

FRIDA: That's hateful.

AUGUST: No, hate is the mastery of the cleaver.

>(FRIDA is writing. A spotlight picks up STRINDBERG.)

STRINDBERG: It was my heart, my heart that was cut out!

>(STRINDBERG begins to choke himself to death.)

FRIDA: August, no!

>(STRINDBERG falls back upon the divan. His body heaves for breath. The spot fades.)

>August, August... are you alright?

>(Pause.)

AUGUST: Yes... I think so. (Short pause.) I see... I have... fatigued you. Sometimes I go on talking for hours without realizing... you see, it has been... it has been a very long time since I have been able to share... (Short pause.) I think I should see you home now, Miss... Miss...?

FRIDA: Uhl... Frida Uhl.

AUGUST: Frida Uhl. (Short pause.) Shall we...?

FRIDA: Where will you go… after you see me home?

AUGUST: There is a tavern named Das Kloster. (Laughs.) I've given it the nickname Zum schwarzen Ferkel.

FRIDA: The Black Pig?

AUGUST: Oink, oink. Home-away-from-home for all the exiled writers, artists, and actors. I am the center—

FRIDA: Don't go there.

AUGUST: But you see, my friends—

FRIDA: Not tonight. Please, don't go there tonight, but, please, August, straight home to your hotel.

AUGUST: I don't understand.

FRIDA: I would like this night to be remembered tomorrow as… our evening together. Please.

AUGUST: I have something for you.

(AUGUST digs into the bag and finds what looks like a package of meat, wrapped in butcher's paper and tied with twine.)

Here. Take it, it's yours.

(FRIDA takes the package.)

FRIDA: Something… what is it? Meat? What?

AUGUST: Open it!

FRIDA: Herr Strindberg, what is it?

AUGUST: My heart.

FRIDA: Your heart.

AUGUST: Yes.

FRIDA: Oh no. (Laughs.) No no no no no. Take it back, please, at once.

AUGUST: Very well.

(AUGUST takes the package.)

I don't mean to make a fool of you.

FRIDA: Of course you wouldn't.

(AUGUST puts the package back into the bag.)

AUGUST: I, I must know what kind of creature you are really. (Short pause.) I would like... to walk by your side, always, forever, beneath the trees, beside the sea. (Short pause.) Believe me, precious child, tonight, in the library of Otto Neumann-Hofer, you did, indeed, hold in your most compassionate hands the actual physical heart of August Strindberg.

(End of scene.)

Scene Three. The Apartment.

(A door. A screen. Two chairs. A table with a typewriter and a telephone. FRIDA is changing out of her evening gown. Her sister MITZI sits on a chair, knitting. She is about thirty years old and dresses like a matron, darkly.)

FRIDA: Sister, I am living like a writer, not like a schoolgirl. And the word 'flirt' applies to a lieutenant of the Guards, not to August Strindberg.

MITZI: The people you meet are no good for marrying.

FRIDA: Who said anything about getting married?

MITZI: The basic purpose in life for a young woman is to catch a husband.

FRIDA: Then I have no purpose. Oh, Mitzi, help me with this.

> (MITZI helps FRIDA from the gown.)

Look how society expects us to dress: Up here, flesh, vulnerability, touch-me-not frigidity. No wonder a man won't look me in the face. But down here, where we throb, corsets, iron.

MITZI: Frida.

FRIDA: What? Doesn't every woman have a wild beast inside? Perhaps mine is the wildest of all.

MITZI: You're playing with fire.

FRIDA: That's the game. Insane. We're lapdogs who do our tricks and get petted for it.

MITZI: Your expectations of life are excessive. There.

FRIDA: Thank you. (Short pause.) Except for my instincts, I would have made a dozen unfortunate marriages by now.

> (FRIDA goes behind a screen and changesinto a stylish business suit.)

MITZI: Vienna is literally bursting with good, decent, well-placed, eligible bachelors.

FRIDA: Austrian men. Emptiness and tantrums.

MITZI: What did you talk about, with this Strindberg?

FRIDA: Philosophy, psychology, biology, geometry, chemistry, botany, astronomy, theology, languages, literature… also about him. He's the son of a servant and a Viking. He can be quite wild, fierce. But gentle, too. He blushes like a newborn baby. His mouth, his lips, and his eyes are wonderful. His hair flames. His brain flashes like a scalpel. He's a disciple of

Nietzsche, and yet his own man, I think.

MITZI: What in heaven's name does that mean?

FRIDA: The superman now accepts the superwoman as an equal in the struggle for power.

MITZI: Frida… marry a man, not a monkey.

FRIDA: An unusual artistic woman must be allowed to practice unusual artistic morals.

(FRIDA steps from behind the screen.)

MITZI: Frida, what are you doing dressed like that? You've got to get to bed.

FRIDA: Mitzi, I have a deadline.

MITZI: But we're catching the six o'clock train to Vienna.

FRIDA: Not we, you.

MITZI: Papa is expecting you.

FRIDA: Father is going to be disappointed then, isn't he?

(FRIDA goes to the typewriter, puts a piece of paper into the cylinder.)

MITZI: Papa is offering you two alternatives: return to mother, or take up residence immediately in Munich, where the opportunity for open rebellion is less likely.

(FRIDA is typing.)

I recommend mother.

FRIDA: Pooh.

MITZI: Frida, there is a point beyond which you must not go, or you will run

39

up against a wall. Papa will crush you.

(FRIDA is typing. MITZI rips the paper out of the machine and tears it in two.)

Obey.

(FRIDA bursts into tears.)

Frida, stop it. Stop it.

FRIDA: If I were to disappear from the face of the earth, you wouldn't miss me. The real me you wouldn't miss at all. I'm a stranger to all of you.

MITZI: Stop crying and put on the mask. No woman dares to show her true face. Put on the mask.

FRIDA: The supermodern, which I have become, does not believe in masks, only hunger, thirst... hunger and thirst.

(End of scene.)

Scene Four. The Black Pig.

(Tables and chairs. A piano. STACHU plays the piano as the scene opens. He wears a dirty red velvet jacket and working-man's trousers. AUGUST is drinking at one of the tables.)

STACHU: (sings) I lay in a dusky thicket of thorns—
But I was not afraid—
Because in the shadows before me sat—
An immortal—
A superman—
Strindberg...!

AUGUST: (applauds) Thank you, Stachu, thank you.

STACHU: I love you, father.

(STACHU goes to AUGUST.)

AUGUST: Well, and I love Berlin, and oink, oink, The Black Pig. In my homeland— Sit, sit down, Stachu.

(STACHU sits at the table.)

In my homeland, I am treated like a pariah. Sweden has room only for the
smallest pygmy, but in Berlin one may be a giant, a Hoffman, a Wagner,
a Nietzsche, or or or...

STACHU: A Strindberg.

AUGUST: Yes, even a Strindberg.

STACHU: Father, master, you are the contents of my brain.

(STACHU bursts into tears.)

AUGUST: Stop blubbering, Stachu, and drink. I can't stand it when a man cries.
It's a betrayal of our manly instincts.

STACHU: Yes, father. (Short pause.) Well... how did your evening go with the
esteemed critic, Otto Neumann-Hofer?

AUGUST: The man's a boor, an idiot. I totally avoided his company.

STACHU: But is that not suicide?

AUGUST: Certainly, and why not? Do you think I find life so amusing?

STACHU: Then you've no right to lament your fate. It is you who stand in your
own way.

AUGUST: Life has taught me that however crazy my behavior, things always
turn out right in the end. And whenever I use my reason, things go wrong.

STACHU: Fatalist.

AUGUST: Life is meaningless.

STACHU: What did you do all evening then... flirt with the ladies?

AUGUST: I did talk to one about my scientific experiments.

STACHU: How old was she?

AUGUST: Oh, nineteen or twenty.

STACHU: You dog. Was she beautiful?

AUGUST: (shrugs) Since my divorce, I'm afraid, one woman looks like any other to me.

STACHU: Was she... (Laughs.) You know...

AUGUST: If she were to walk in here this very moment with a female companion, I couldn't tell you which one I have spent the evening with in intimate conversation and which one is a perfect stranger. (Short pause.) What is a woman anyway? No more than a bird's nest for man's eggs.

STACHU: Man's eggs? An interesting theory.

AUGUST: One needs only a constant temperature of thirty-seven degrees, a suitable nourishment fluid, and a Petri dish. Then man will be emancipated. Completely.

STACHU: You ought to fall in love, master.

AUGUST: And betray my right hand? Never. (Laughs.) A year's celibacy has almost made me an epileptic, but no no... no new bonds. I can't take that.

STACHU: Oh, love! Everything turns upside down. You see new depths, climb new heights. My god, how superb, walk across the sky, light your cigaret with the sun. (Sings.) 'All my money gone...' (Short pause.) I tremble... therefore I love... ahh—

AUGUST: Enough of that.

STACHU: Women drive me crazy!

AUGUST: Let's have another drink.

(STACHU pours two drinks.)

STACHU: Skaal!

AUGUST: Skaal!

(They drink.)

STACHU: This is how life should always be.

(STACHU pours more drinks.)

AUGUST: I once heard a member of a writer's group express exactly the same sentiment in the same words, and before the night was over, all its members were deadly enemies.

STACHU: Do you believe that you and I could ever be enemies?

AUGUST: What, the Poles and the Swedes? We were born enemies.

STACHU: No! You are my father. You've taught me all I know about writing.

(STACHU leans on AUGUST.)

AUGUST: (laughing) My ancestors were savages.

STACHU: (kissing) I kiss your hands, father... I kiss...

AUGUST: Stachu, stop it. Let go. Stop kissing.

STACHU: Kiss your ten fingers... kiss...

AUGUST: I can't stand to get my hands wet.

(AUGUST throws STACHU down on the floor.)

Argh! (Laughs.) I feel an immense need to turn savage and create a new world.

(STACHU gets up. He throws down a key.)

STACHU: Here... the key to my apartment. You... you must go to my apartment. You... you must sleep with my Maschka, my mistress—

(A spotlight picks up STRINDBERG.)

STRINDBERG: Argh!

(STRINDBERG jumps on STACHU, and they fall to the floor. They roll around, fighting and wrestling.)

Life is Hell, a punishment!

STACHU: You and no other, my father.

STRINDBERG: My dear friend should be my worst enemy.

STACHU: I will share my Maschka.

STRINDBERG: My beloved should be my hated.

STACHU: She's always so pleased to see you.

STRINDBERG: Everything is worthless.

STACHU: I insist. You must accept my key.

STRINDBERG: If only I could rest my brain.

STACHU: Make love to my mistress.

STRINDBERG: Buddha offered his body...

STACHU: You'll be doing me...

STRINDBERG: Offered his body to the tiger.

STACHU: Doing me a great favor.

>   (The spot fades. End of scene.)

Scene Five. The Swing.

>   (FRIDA and MITZI sit together on a swing.)

FRIDA: Oh, I'm shivering.

MITZI: My dear, dear Frida. My dear, dear little girl.

FRIDA: Do you know that picture of me on father's desk, a portrait made centuries ago it seems?

MITZI: You were fifteen.

FRIDA: A wooden figure, bony shoulders, the arms long and skinny. None of that is me anymore, though my waist is still twenty-two-and-a-half inches. Impressive, isn't it? But the face is the same. Was I ever a child? Was I ever happy?

MITZI: You were a beautiful child.

FRIDA: Take a good look the next time you see it. Nothing but devil's tricks, a foolish waste of paint and gold leaf and ivory, nothing but false trash.

MITZI: My sweet and precious little girl, my precious little girl.

>   (Pause.)

FRIDA: I do love you, Mitzi.

MITZI: And we love you.

>   (MITZI gets off the swing.)

Well, off to bed, shall we now? We do have an early train.

FRIDA: No, I'm not going.

(FRIDA swings alone.)

MITZI: What's your choice, Frida? Munich or mother?

FRIDA: Neither. I refuse to do what father wishes. I'll cause a scandal first. I swear it.

MITZI: Life is not a fairy tale. The future is not a toy.

(Pause.)

What will I tell Papa?

FRIDA: Tell him…

(Pause.)

Tell him…

(Pause.)

He can read about it in the papers.

(FRIDA swings higher. End of scene.)

Scene Six. The Black Pig.

(AUGUST and STACHU are wrestling on the floor. EDVARD, dressed in a dark, conservative suit, tie askew, sits at the table drinking their drinks.)

STACHU: Edzin! (Short pause.) Father, Edzin is here.

(They stop fighting.)

AUGUST: Munch! Can't you afford to buy yourself a drink?

EDVARD: Kiss my ass, Strindberg.

(STACHU and AUGUST join him.)

STACHU: Edzin, old boy, what's the matter?

EDVARD: My exhibition… the pictures A Frieze of Life have caused a tremendous uproar. The police were called in. The critics want to boycott the gallery.

STACHU: But, but… how can they do this?

EDVARD: One critic in particular, the kind who if he had a chance would shovel manure into the lap of the Madonna, he made the most noise of all.

STACHU: Your paintings, Edzin, spring from that moment when reason has become… silent… when, when…

EDVARD: He was the hopeless cross between a bad painter and an impossible critic—

AUGUST: Critics, bah…!

STACHU: Your paintings… your paintings are chemical preparations of the soul.

EDVARD: Look at Michelangelo. Is the Sistine Chapel wallpaper?

STACHU: The noises of the present give way to the voices of the future.

EDVARD: A work of art has to come from within. It must.

STACHU: Art, glorious art! What else sustains us in the face of all failure, insult and hatred?

AUGUST: Mother.

EDVARD: God damn! Some ass or other paints three sheep in a potato field, or three potatoes in a sheep pasture... or maybe three peasants shoveling potatoes into a manure spreader, and voila! He gets money for it... and a gold medal. (Short pause.) I paint humanity... close. Real close. I paint the human soul, at the opening where a monster crawls out of the depths. I paint that abomination, that eternal beauty... and what do I get? The crowd laughs all the way from Paris to Berlin. I get the police. (Short pause.) The brutal masses demand freshly slaughtered young painters for breakfast... something to spread on their bread.

AUGUST: Bah bah bah...!

STACHU: What do you mean... bah?

AUGUST: Bah bah bah... When one is untrue to oneself, the result is always shit. Learn this, you two: Life is a great butcher... active, dangerous, arbitrary, horrible. (Short pause.) Stretch your bleeding canvas, Munch—

EDVARD: You don't know anything about painting.

AUGUST: What's that you're saying, something stupid again?

EDVARD: If you throw a stone at a group of boys, they will run apart... an action. That's composition. You don't know the first thing about it.

AUGUST: I'm merely recognized as the outstanding Scandinavian painter of the modern epoch.

EDVARD: You?

AUGUST: I am.

EDVARD: If that's true, then I must be equally renowned as the outstanding playwright.

AUGUST: I didn't know you could read, let alone write.

STACHU: Gentlemen, gentlemen... it's time to blow the backs of our heads across the street.

(STACHU pours drinks all round.)

Skaal!

AUGUST: Skaal!

EDVARD: Skaal!

(All drink.)

STACHU: Let's have another.

(STACHU pours drinks.)

Skaal!

AUGUST: Skaal!

EDVARD: Skaal!

(All drink. Pause.)

I was hoping to sell a few paintings so I could afford to get married.

STACHU: What's this? You, Edzin, who believe in free love?

AUGUST: (laughing) Is she emancipated, too?

EDVARD: As a matter of fact, she is. We intend to marry the world.

AUGUST: Jealousy will be your best man, then.

STACHU: Who is she, Edzin, who is she? Who who who?

EDVARD: Well, her name is… Dagny. Dagny Juell.

AUGUST: Did you say Uhl?

STACHU: No, he said Juell… Dagny Juell.

EDVARD: She's a Norwegian pianist studying here in Berlin. She's from a good family, too. My father knows her father quite well—

STACHU: When do we meet her? Edzin, when?

EDVARD: Well, I can't very well ask her to come here.

STACHU: Why not? (Short pause.) Edzin…?

AUGUST: (laughs) The free lover is afraid of the Swede. I'll steal his bride.

EDVARD: I'm not afraid of you, Strindberg.

STACHU: Is she beautiful, Edzin?

AUGUST: It's a long and ancient tradition in Sweden, stealing brides.

STACHU: Has she read my novel? (Short pause.) Well, has she?

AUGUST: He's afraid I'll fuck her.

(EDVARD jumps up and kicks his chair away.)

EDVARD: I'm not afraid of you or anyone.

(EDVARD puts up his fists.)

Come on, mother lover, come on.

(A spotlight on STRINDBERG who jumps up and kicks his chair away.)

STRINDBERG: Butcher!

(Pause.)

STACHU: Gentlemen, please, gentlemen.

(STACHU pours drinks all round.)

Skaal!

(No one moves.)

Father. Brother. (Short pause.) We are all friends here.

(No one moves.)

Friends.

(No one moves. The spot fades. End of scene.)

Scene Seven. The Bedroom.

(A bed, a trunk, a chair, a mirror, a door. STRINDBERG lies rigidly on the bed. It is night. A dreamlike WRAITH is present in the room. A spotlight picks up STRINDBERG, and he sits bolt upright in bed.)

STRINDBERG: (chanting) If I commit no wrong, I've nothing to fear. If I commit no wrong, I've nothing to fear.

(Pause. STRINDBERG addresses the WRAITH.)

Do you know why flowers grow out of filth? Do you? Because flowers don't like filth, so they hurry as fast as they can up toward the light, to bloom, and to die.

(Pause.)

Following my divorce, stripped of furniture, family, future, I took a room in a cheap hotel. A mysterious stranger was living in the room adjacent to my writing desk, and evidently he too was a writer, because, curiously, whenever I was writing, I could hear him writing on the other side of the wall. When I paused to scratch my head, I could hear him scratching his head. When I yawned, I could hear him yawning. (Short pause.) This went on for three days. On the third night, as I was going to bed, I could hear him going to bed, too, but he was going to bed not in the room next to my desk, but in the room on the other side… the room next to my bed. (Short pause.) Yes, he was.

(Pause.)

I could hear him lying there, stretched out parallel to me. I picked up a book to read. I could hear him turning the pages of a book. I blew out my lamp, turned over and tried to go to sleep. He blew out his lamp, turned over and, twins, breathing on two sides of a wall, we shared the sleepless night. (Chants.) If I commit no wrong, I've nothing to fear. If I commit no wrong, I've nothing to fear. If I commit no wrong… (Short pause.) Commit no wrong? Now that's hard. That is so hard. Isn't it? Well?

(STRINDBERG gets out of bed and goes downstage toward a large stove or furnace.)

In an effort to avoid the stranger, my secret twin living on both sides of my room at once… how does he do that? I willfully determined to abandon literature and never to fall asleep. Confining my activities to the center of the room only, I decided to seek truth in alchemy, to make gold with the aid of fire. I procured a furnace, crucibles, charcoal, bellows, tongs.

(STRINDBERG prepares an experiment. The fire roars up.)

Stripped to the waist like a smith, I sweated in front of an open fire.

(Smoke pours out of the furnace.)

Sparrows… sparrows had built a nest in the flue of the chimney… and the fumes… the fumes and smoke filled the tiny room… giving me a terrible headache. (Short pause.) After the third remelting, I was furious with my work and cursed my fate. Have I burned truth in the fire? Have I roasted flesh? Have I eaten evil? I looked at the borax in the crucible, and a tiny skull with two tiny red eyes stared back—

(A DOPPLEGANGER leaps from the furnace and attacks STRINDBERG with a knife. Pause.)

If I commit no wrong, I've nothing to fear. If I commit no wrong…

(The spot fades. End of scene.)

Scene Eight. The Apartment.

(FRIDA, dressed in a kimono, is taking tea with the morning papers. The telephone rings, and she answers.)

FRIDA: (on the phone) Good morning. (Short pause.) Papa!

(Pause.)

Mitzi left hours ago. (Short pause.) I live in Berlin.

(Pause.)

You're a newspaperman. Don't be so naive as to believe everything you read. You can't hold me responsible for a typographical error. (Laughs.) Deny everything.

(Pause.)

Yes of course, Mitzi is perfection, and I am a monster. And this mess, as you put it, this mess I've gotten myself into is the unavoidable result of my relationship to modern literature, don't you agree?

(Pause.)

No, no, Dada, Dada, no.

(Pause.)

No! I won't go. I'll spread all the more violently the rumors. (Short pause.) I won't, I won't, I won't—

(FRIDA hangs up. A long pause. FRIDA goes to

the typewriter and begins to type.)

Break... with... Papa... inevitable.

(She types. End of scene.)

Scene Nine. The Bedroom.

(AUGUST lies sleeping on the bed, his head hanging over the edge to the floor. He awakes from a nightmare.)

AUGUST: Mommy!

(Someone begins to pound on the other side of the door. It is STACHU.)

STACHU: Father... Father... Father... Father... Father...

AUGUST: Oh, bah, enter!

STACHU: (still knocking) Father... Father...

AUGUST: Enter and abandon all hope!

(STACHU bursts through the door. He has a newspaper.)

STACHU: Father...

AUGUST: Stop calling me Father. It reminds me I had three children and have them no more.

STACHU: Are you alright?

AUGUST: I, I shall live, but tell me... Am I insane, or is the world turned upon its head today?

STACHU: You are upside-down, master, hanging over the edge of your bed.

AUGUST: Oh.

(Rights himself.)

Good. Thank you. I feel great. Absolutely buoyant.

STACHU: I'm not surprised.

(Flaunts the newspaper.)

Congratulations… on your engagement. It's in all the papers.

AUGUST: Ha, what did I tell you last night, about fate? So, the Resident Theatre is doing my comedy after all. Good old Neumann-Ofer—

STACHU: No no no. (Short pause.) You… are to be wed.

AUGUST: Wed, did you say?

STACHU: Yes.

AUGUST: I'd sooner drink poison. It's quicker.

STACHU: Here's the paper—

(AUGUST snatches the paper.)

Right there.

AUGUST: (reads aloud) 'Literary Berlin is abuzz trying to guess which Viennese beauty has secretly agreed to become August Strindberg's second wife'…? (Short pause.) Lies. Scandal. Compromise. Who wrote this trash? (Short pause.) Frida Uhl…? Never heard of her.

(STACHU has an envelope.)

STACHU: Well… (Coughs.) On my way up to your room, the front desk handed me an envelope. (Sniffs.) A perfumed envelope. The return address is a Miss Frida Uhl—

55

(AUGUST snatches the envelope.)

AUGUST: Give it up.

(Tears it open. There's a note.)

STACHU: First Munch, now you. Soon my Maschka and I will be the only set of free lovers in the entire city of Berlin.

AUGUST: (reads aloud) 'Respectfully request your presence at eight, as a guest in my apartment. Frida Uhl.' (Short pause.) What time is it?

STACHU: April in Berlin. The lime trees are in blossom.

AUGUST: Can you be more precise?

STACHU: Three minutes past seven o'clock.

AUGUST: Morning or night?

STACHU: Evening, my master, sweet with lilacs.

(AUGUST opens the trunk and pulls out a small guitar. He strums it once or twice. It's horribly out of tune.)

Oh...! Did you have to do that?

AUGUST: Well, I'm off then.

STACHU: Armed with a guitar?

AUGUST: Thrust into the spectacle of pursuing a romance in public, I must appear to be the aggressor. My manhood demands it.

STACHU: It's every man's duty to have a high opinion of himself.

(AUGUST at the mirror.)

AUGUST: Oh, frightful.

(He attempts to neaten and straighten himself.)

So much for that.

(Turns around.)

Stachu... a hug.

(AUGUST and STACHU embrace.)

STACHU: Shall we rendezvous at The Black Pig?

AUGUST: Midnight! I'll bring you up to date on my conquest.

STACHU: Munch is bringing his fianceé whom he claims resembles a four-teenth-century Madonna.

(AUGUST has the guitar and his green bag.)

AUGUST: Women.

(He exits. Pause.)

STACHU: Father... wait. I'm going, too.

(STACHU starts for an exit but comes back for his newspaper. He exits.)

Father...

(Pause. STRINDBERG crawls out from beneath the bed as a spotlight picks him up.)

STRINDBERG: Now I know all the pain of being. I miss things I never valued, regret wrongs I didn't commit.

(He rummages through the trunk.)

Insults, shame, sham, humiliation. This double-goer, shadow brother, doppelganger pretender. Mustard yellow frock coats. Silk scarves. Beaver hats. (Short pause.) Perfumed peacock!

(Pause.)

I never knew the lucky ease of the favorite but hurled myself tenaciously into life. I learned the lightning attack of the mink and the wolverine. The tasks of dog, cat, rat, any domestic creature, I could never fully comprehend. To live by the opium of the mundane, it wasn't for me.

(Pause.)

My memory, all of it, and my prophecy, all of it, now gather together in my brain. My head is about to explode like an electric accumulator. Beware, Strindberg-pretender.

(He finds an axe at the bottom of the trunk.)

You are the victim now, the new sacrifice. I am the superman.

(The spot fades. End of scene.)

Scene Ten. The Apartment.

(A spotlight picks up STRINDBERG breaking down the door with his axe. Off, a doorbell rings. STRINDBERG hides behind a curtain. FRIDA enters in her kimono and smoking a cigaret.)

FRIDA: Hello...? Who's there?

(AUGUST, with his guitar and green bag, appears in the broken doorway.)

So, it's you.

(FRIDA notices the broken door.)

Feeling a little wild tonight?

AUGUST: (bowing) Good evening, mademoiselle.

FRIDA: Have you come to take revenge?

AUGUST: Take revenge? On you? What could possibly have given you that idea?

FRIDA: Well, I am only a silly schoolgirl.

AUGUST: Did you not want me to come? How strange, but this afternoon I fancied you were calling to me telepathically.

FRIDA: Of course I wished you would come.

AUGUST: There you see, I knew it.

FRIDA: I requested it, but… did you get my note? Please do come in.

AUGUST: Thank you. (Short pause.) You are smoking.

FRIDA: You don't approve?

AUGUST: I once wrote a monograph proving one may cure all illnesses with tobacco.

FRIDA: Is that so?

(Sticks out her tongue. Puts out the cigaret.)

AUGUST: Yes, but that's another subject. I want to ask you, madame, mademoiselle, how you happen to be here, this city and this year? (Short pause.) We are all, I suspect, in quest of her.

FRIDA: Her, Herr Strindberg?

AUGUST: Mother. (Short pause.) My own mother died when I was still a small child.

FRIDA: I'm so sorry to hear that.

AUGUST: A desolate longing for mother has been with me all my life.

FRIDA: You poor man. Oh, Herr Strindberg...

>   (AUGUST gets down on his knees.)

AUGUST: I beg, down on hands and knees, please call me August.

FRIDA: Tell me more about yourself... August?

>   (AUGUST jumps to his feet, strums the guitar.)

AUGUST: First, I should like to share an original composition on the guitar. (Strumming.) I am currently in the process of developing entirely new principles for the tuning of guitars.

>   (He adjusts the strings. Meanwhile, an arm emerges from behind the curtain and fishes for the green bag abandoned nearby.)

Faultlessly tuned instruments run the risk of a too regular beauty which falsifies reality. In life, nothing is ever absolutely in tune. In fact, imperfection is the charm of life, don't you agree?

FRIDA: Well, I do enjoy a good melody.

AUGUST: Life is an eternal fragment. We don't remember its beginning and cannot guess the end.

FRIDA: You are going to play something?

AUGUST: Yes.

>   (AUGUST stands on one leg.)

One moment of quiet meditation.

>   (The moment passes. AUGUST, still balanced on one leg, begins to play and sing.)

'My mother groaned—
My father wept—
Into the dangerous world I leapt—
Helpless, naked, piping loud—
Like a fiend hid in a cloud—
Struggling with my father's hands—
Striving against my swaddling bands—
Bound and weary I thought best—
To sulk upon my mother's breast—'

(AUGUST plays a final flourish.)

FRIDA: (applauds) August, wonderful!

AUGUST: Thank you. My pleasure.

FRIDA: Did you write the verse as well?

AUGUST: William Blake. I've given up the pen myself.

FRIDA: You've… given up your livelihood?

AUGUST: Slaughterhood would be a better word. Writing. What an occupation. Spy out your neighbor's secrets, betray your brother's birthmark, use one's own wife as an experimental rabbit, behave like a beast, chop, burn, defile. And then, yes, then to expect everyone to buy back the remains in the form of a book. Shame, shame. I've killed the artist in me. I'll never write another word.

> (Meanwhile, the arm behind the curtain is in possession of the green bag. The hand opens the bag, removes the wrapped package, and disappears with it behind the curtain.)

FRIDA: One must be practical.

AUGUST: Yes, mustn't one now, Miss Uhl…?

> (Pause.)

FRIDA: Have... have you read my journalism?

AUGUST: I have. This morning's edition if I'm not mistaken.

(Pause.)

FRIDA: Well then, there's only one thing one can do.

(FRIDA produces a small round black bomb with a fuse. She lights it.)

AUGUST: What are you doing?

FRIDA: Blowing us up.

AUGUST: But why?

FRIDA: To free the world from poverty and oppression.

AUGUST: Can't we discuss this further over dinner?

FRIDA: You only want to fatten me for the butcher.

(AUGUST gets down on his knees and shuffles over to FRIDA.)

Man must be brought down from his pedestal. Let him learn to walk again on earth.

AUGUST: Oh, please, please, I beg. I beg.

(AUGUST nuzzles his head in FRIDA's crotch. Pause. She brings her free hand down upon his head. Pause.)

FRIDA: Very well.

(FRIDA hands the bomb to AUGUST, and he snuffs it out.)

AUGUST: Merciful maiden.

FRIDA: I am a regular habitueé of a nice little restaurant in the Tiergarten. Shall we?

AUGUST: Whatever you require.

FRIDA: I must change.

(FRIDA exits.)

AUGUST: I'll arrange for a cab and wait below.

(AUGUST gathers his guitar and green bag. He notices the bag
has been opened. He looks inside. The arm emerges and grabs
him around the throat. AUGUST chokes and struggles. He
reaches into his tux, produces the dagger and stabs behind
him into the curtain. We hear a groan and a body hits the floor
as the package rolls out into the room. AUGUST picks it up and
puts it back into the green bag. He exits quickly through the
broken door. Pause. STRINDBERG crawls out from behind the
curtain. His tux is red with blood. A spotlight picks him up as
he crawls to the door.)

STRINDBERG: I am... I am... August Strindberg. I am... I am... the super...
super...

(The spot fades. End of scene.)

(End of Act One. Interval.)

Act Two

Scene One. The Streets of Berlin.

> (A spotlight picks up STRINDBERG. He is crawling down the street. He is sick, cold, and wounded. The spot fades. End of scene.)

Scene Two. The Restaurant.

> (A table and two chairs. Napkins, wine glasses, a rose in a vase. On the scene is a WAITER, formerly dressed but also wearing a bloody butcher's apron. AUGUST and FRIDA enter.)

AUGUST: May I...? (Short pause.) Your wrap in positively electrical.

FRIDA: My father has many friends. Imagine, this leopard died for me.

> (FRIDA wears a skintight, transparent green dress.)

AUGUST: Mon dieu, what a dress.

FRIDA: I see you like transparent green.

AUGUST: It clings to your body like a snakeskin.

FRIDA: It hisses like a snake when I walk.

> (FRIDA leads the way to the table.)

Hear it? Green leaves, yellow sun, joy of life, come, follow.

AUGUST: Eros! Now I'm lost.

(AUGUST follows FRIDA. They sit at the table.)

FRIDA: Ludwig!

(The WAITER approaches.)

LUDWIG: Mademoiselle.

FRIDA: Hors d'oeuvres.

AUGUST: Black eggs and oysters.

FRIDA: The very best, s'il vous plait. My guest is a Swedish gentleman, Europe's greatest playwright.

LUDWIG: Ah, yes. Welcome, monsieur. I knew immediately you were no ordinary gentleman.

FRIDA: August, what would we like for a main course… lobster, chicken?

(AUGUST and FRIDA look at each other. A long pause.)

We aren't hungry, then?

AUGUST: Roses and wine.

FRIDA: Ludwig, a bottle of chianti.

(LUDWIG bows and exits. Pause.)

AUGUST: So what's your big secret all about?

FRIDA: Do I have a secret?

AUGUST: Yes. The secret which you are about to tell me.

FRIDA: Well… yes. My father has ordered me to leave Berlin at once.

AUGUST: Oh?

FRIDA: Yes.

AUGUST: Soon?

FRIDA: At once, to my father, means very soon. Tomorrow.

AUGUST: Well, that is very soon.

FRIDA: Yes.

AUGUST: Where are you to go?

FRIDA: Father has commanded me to leave Berlin at once and to return either to mother or to Munich. He believes the Berlin air is poisoned, that I am the model for the young woman who kills her father in the new play by Hermann Sudermann. (Short pause.) But I don't want to leave Berlin. Not now, August. What shall I tell him?

AUGUST: Tell him that he is behind the times.

FRIDA: What do you mean?

AUGUST: I mean... Sudermann left for Italy a week ago, and Strindberg is now in Berlin.

FRIDA: I can't tell him that.

AUGUST: Then... I shall miss your companionship.

FRIDA: Come, too.

AUGUST: What, to your mother?

FRIDA: No, Munich.

AUGUST: You mean it?

FRIDA: Yes, do come. Do.

AUGUST: Do you know, I cannot think of one reason why not.

FRIDA: Indeed.

AUGUST: It, it doesn't really matter where I live if...

FRIDA: If?

AUGUST: If I may be near to you.

> (AUGUST and FRIDA look at each other. Long pause. End of scene.)

Scene Three. The Black Pig.

> (STACHU is playing the piano. EDVARD and DAGNY are at a table drinking absinthe. DAGNY is a dirty blonde in a dull-grey baggy dress.)

STACHU: (sings) 'I saw the sun—
And then I saw the hidden one—
The hidden one—
The hidden one beyond the sun who sang'—
Let's mend the broken world—
Shivering with pain—
Loneliness and sorrow—
Weeping in the rain—
Let's bend the broken world—
And make it round again—

EDVARD: Stachu. Stachu. Come here. Stachu.

STACHU: (playing) Edzin. Yes, I see you. Hello.

> (STACHU finishes with a wild flourish. He goes to their table.)

Well, and so, Edzin, you, I see, have brought a friend.

EDVARD: This is her, my fianceé.

STACHU: Hello.

EDVARD: Dagny, my best friend in all the world… Stachu.

DAGNY: So, that's you. (Laughs.)

STACHU: Yes, it's I, Stanislaw Przybyszewski. Nothing unusual, as you see. And you're… Dagny Juell.

DAGNY: Yes.

(STACHU and DAGNY shake hands.)

I think you're beautiful. (Laughs.)

EDVARD: She likes you, Stachu. I've been telling her everything about you.

STACHU: Well, I hope not quite everything. (Laughs.) Coming from Edzin, you must have expected some strange sort of animal.

DAGNY: But you are a beautiful, wild animal. (Laughs.)

EDVARD: She has the idea that in Poland the bears regularly visit people's houses to lick out the pots and pans.

STACHU: Well, not quite.

EDVARD: She knows all the stories of when we were poor artists sharing a room in Paris. (Laughs.) The time we got the landlord drunk, remember? He had to crawl home on all fours.

STACHU: (laughing) Yes, and he'd lost his key, so he knocked a hole through the window with his head.

EDVARD: (laughing) Yes, yes. (Short pause.) And the time we were so poor we only owned one pair of trousers between us? Whenever you attended lectures at the Sorbonne, I had to paint in my underwear. (Laughs.) My god, it was cold sometimes.

DAGNY: You painted in your underwear?

EDVARD: Yes, yes. Didn't I, Stachu?

DAGNY: You must have looked uglier than a stork.

EDVARD: I suppose I did. (To STACHU.) Isn't she devastatingly attractive? And so bold, progressive too.

DAGNY: Edzin, enough.

STACHU: (to DAGNY) I understand you are studying for a career as a concert pianist.

EDVARD: She's also an adept in literature, and the visual arts. (Short pause.) As you can see, we are both madly in love.

DAGNY: You mustn't bore Mister Przybyszewski with such uninteresting speculations.

STACHU: (laughs) She's certainly got you well trained.

DAGNY: (to EDVARD) Go get me another drink.

EDVARD: But I just bought you a litre of absinthe.

> (DAGNY pours the last of the litre into her glass and drinks it down.)

DAGNY: Go get me another drink.

EDVARD: (to STACHU) She's a feminist and a bohemian. Drinks absinthe by the litre and never gets drunk. I'll be right back.

> (EDVARD exits. Pause.)

DAGNY: I'm insane with jealously of you.

STACHU: Of me?

72

DAGNY: Edzin never stops talking about you. Stachu is this. Stachu is that. Stachu, Stachu, is all I hear.

STACHU: But you've no reason to be jealous—

DAGNY: I shall go mad, I know, unless... (Laughs.)

STACHU: Unless? (Short pause.) Well? Unless?

(Pause.)

Now I shall go mad unless you finish your sentence.

DAGNY: Do you believe that one should conquer one's desires?

STACHU: Well, once I had a friend who did.

DAGNY: Oh? Was he a saint?

STACHU: Well, you see, he had his heart set on seeing Rome, and so one day he set off on foot, determined to walk all the way to Rome from Poland. Yes, and he got within one mile of his destination, then he turned back, saying, 'A man should be able to conquer his desires.' (Short pause.) Of course upon reaching home again, he went insane.

(STACHU and DAGNY laugh.)

So what desire is driving you mad?

DAGNY: I want to sleep with you.

(EDVARD enters with a litre of absinthe.)

EDVARD: This should keep us happy.

(He sits down.)

So what have you two been up to?

STACHU: Dagny and I have become... comrades.

73

DAGNY: Comrades? You and I?

STACHU: Yes, certainly.

EDVARD: Congratulations. I knew you'd like each other.

DAGNY: I have never had a friend who was also a man.

(Pause.)

EDVARD: Well, in three weeks, more or less—

DAGNY: More or less—

EDVARD: He'll be our best man, too. Won't you, Stachu?

(Pause.)

I'm so happy. My best friend... my fianceé.

(EDVARD pours drinks for everyone.)

You're both so good to me, and we make no demands on one another. Shall we drink? Skaal?

DAGNY: Yes. Let's drink to no demands.

EDVARD: No demands. (Short pause.) Stachu?

STACHU: No demands.

(EDVARD drinks. DAGNY and STACHU look at each other.)

EDVARD: Well...

(Pause.)

Well...

(Pause.)

The human soul is a curious enigma.

(End of scene.)

Scene Four. The Restaurant.

(LUDWIG pours a sample of wine.)

FRIDA: The dark hot blood of southern grapes.

(AUGUST drinks.)

AUGUST: Excellent.

(LUDWIG pours two glasses of wine.)

FRIDA: That will be all, Ludwig.

(LUDWIG bows and exits.)

What shall we drink to, August?

AUGUST: What were we just now talking about, a little while ago before the interruption?

FRIDA: You were saying you might enjoy seeing Munich.

AUGUST: I did say something like that, didn't I? So let's drink to that.

(AUGUST and FRIDA drink.)

FRIDA: Munich is a very daring city, August. The theatrical prospects for modern dramatists are excellent. Ibsen lives there.

AUGUST: Ibsen? Where, in a doll's house? While I stumble through heaven and hell?

FRIDA: I will learn Swedish and translate all your works—

AUGUST: I've been his victim for ten years! Paris! London! Rome! If I move to Munich, I'll no doubt find sufficient lodgings in the cemetery.

FRIDA: Never mind him. He's old. You're new bottles for new wine. How many plays have you unproduced?

AUGUST: Thousands.

FRIDA: Be serious, August. If I'm to be your manager, tell the truth.

AUGUST: (taps his forehead) Up here.

FRIDA: Very well, thousands. You shall make fortunes.

AUGUST: Or at least one fortune, don't you think?

FRIDA: But you must be practical.

AUGUST: That word again. Yes?

FRIDA: Whatever you hope to gain from any play, deduct thirty percent for miscalculation.

AUGUST: Thirty? I always allow ninety percent for miscalculation, sometimes a hundred.

FRIDA: Be sensible, please. This is serious.

AUGUST: I am absolutely serious. It is impossible for a dramatist, who lives by favor of the public, to promise anything. I insist, ninety percent.

FRIDA: Thirty-five.

AUGUST: Eighty.

FRIDA: Forty.

AUGUST: Sixty, and you can have it.

(AUGUST and FRIDA laugh.)

Divine levity.

FRIDA: How happy we are, so free of care.

AUGUST: I hope so.

FRIDA: You hope so, August?

AUGUST: Yes.

(AUGUST opens the green bag and pulls out an old rusty and heavy pistol which obviously cannot be fired. He places it down upon the table.)

FRIDA: What is this?

AUGUST: To our trip.

(He drinks.)

FRIDA: This is meant for our trip?

AUGUST: It depends. I put it in my bag today because I didn't know how this day would go for us.

(FRIDA picks it up.)

FRIDA: This isn't real. It's a prop.

AUGUST: I am not afraid.

(FRIDA puts the gun to her head.)

FRIDA: Bang! (Short pause.) Put this iron horror away. We have every reason to live.

AUGUST: We do?

FRIDA: Of course we do. Don't be coy with me, August. Where's the package?

AUGUST: Package?

FRIDA: Your heart. Surely you've brought it with you tonight.

AUGUST: I have.

FRIDA: It belongs to me now.

AUGUST: Are you talking about free love?

FRIDA: Quite the contrary.

AUGUST: What do you mean?

FRIDA: A supermodern marriage.

AUGUST: Are you mad?

FRIDA: Yes. No. Perhaps.

AUGUST: Which?

FRIDA: What does it matter as long as we are mad and wild and fierce together? (Short pause.) The package.

> (AUGUST puts the gun into the green bag and retrieves the wrapped package. He offers it to FRIDA.)

AUGUST: Will you?

FRIDA: Yes.

> (FRIDA takes the package, looks at it for a moment, then puts it away into her own bag. Pause.)

AUGUST: It is done.

FRIDA: We are lovers.

> (Pause. End of scene.)

Scene Five. The Hotel Room.

> (A bed. A chair. A washstand. A window. The sky is bloodred. DAGNY and STACHU make love like animals.)

STACHU: How has this happened?

DAGNY: Don't ask.

STACHU: I have never before been so in love.

DAGNY: Don't forget.

STACHU: What?

DAGNY: The terms.

STACHU: Terms? What terms?

DAGNY: Tonight, we're lovers. Tomorrow, we're free.

STACHU: No, no. I won't forget. I promise.

> (End of scene.)

Scene Six. The Restaurant.

(At the table, AUGUST has paper and pen.)

AUGUST: Let us compose together the rules of modern marriage.

FRIDA: We two will never be stifled, August?

AUGUST: Never. We shall discover life anew each day. We shall never stand still.

FRIDA: I know nothing about housework.

AUGUST: I don't want you for a wife in order to clean a house. There are maids for that.

FRIDA: I have no talent for diapers.

AUGUST: We shall engage a nurse.

FRIDA: I don't cook.

AUGUST: We shall engage a cook.

FRIDA: Three servants already. But they must be paid, and without my father, I have no money, only debts.

AUGUST: Me, too.

(AUGUST and FRIDA laugh.)

Let's do this. Rule number one. We shall live in three rooms. One for the gentleman…

FRIDA: One for the lady…

AUGUST: Yes. And one for the marriage.

(Pause.)

Rule number two. Catering.

FRIDA: Three. Each to have a door which can be locked.

(Pause.)

AUGUST: Four. One may close the door now and then behind one's own thoughts and feelings.

(Pause.)

FRIDA: Five. One needs time to think of the other person.

(Pause. AUGUST signs with a flourish, then hands the pen and paper to FRIDA.)

AUGUST: Agreed?

FRIDA: Only five rules?

AUGUST: A pentagram of marital bliss.

FRIDA: Agreed

(FRIDA signs.)

AUGUST: Our marriage must never be like, like… like the other. Oh…

(Pause.)

FRIDA: Have you… any news of your children?

AUGUST: Their mother forbids them to write to their father. Can you imagine such a woman?

FRIDA: I would like to see a photo of your children. Have you got one?

AUGUST: Of course I have. Right here. (Short pause.) Well, I thought I had them right on top. Never mind, I'll find them.

(AUGUST rummages in the green bag. LUDWIG enters with a bill. FRIDA pays it. LUDWIG exits. AUGUST finds the photos.)

Here they are.

(Gives the photos to FRIDA.)

FRIDA: Oh, they're beautiful children. How generous you are, August, to give me your children. Who's this?

(AUGUST takes the photo, turns it over.)

AUGUST: That's Karin. She wants to be a teacher. And... this is Greta. She wants to marry and become a mother. And—

FRIDA: He's beautiful.

AUGUST: Hans. He wants to be a chemist doing research to prove his father's theories.

FRIDA: How old is Hans?

AUGUST: Five or six... six.

FRIDA: Do you think we could have him?

AUGUST: Hans?

FRIDA: Yes. Do you think his mother would give him up, and we could raise him?

AUGUST: I don't know. She's a very selfish woman.

FRIDA: The world belongs to the man who has such children.

(AUGUST takes the photos and begins to cry.)

AUGUST: I don't know where they live.

(FRIDA reaches out and touches AUGUST.)

FRIDA: Poor stranger.

(Pause.)

AUGUST: Well, I… I suppose we should go.

FRIDA: Yes, my husband.

(AUGUST puts the photos away. He looks about, taps a spoon against his glass.)

AUGUST: Well, where's the waiter so we can go?

FRIDA: We may go, my husband.

AUGUST: Not until I've paid the bill, we can't.

FRIDA: I invited you, and I paid the bill.

AUGUST: You did?

FRIDA: Yes.

AUGUST: I don't know the customs of Vienna, but here in Berlin, and in Sweden, it's a disgrace for a man to let a lady—

FRIDA: You were my guest.

AUGUST: Don't you understand the sort of reputation you've given me? The names the waiter will hurl upon my back?

FRIDA: Stop acting like a child.

AUGUST: I gave you my heart across this table. You have abused your power and now must expect the usual fate of a tyrant.

FRIDA: What have I done? Does it make any difference whether I entertain at home or in public? What do I… what do we, the super moderns, care for custom or worn-out conventions?

Augustus: My heart. Return it immediately.

Frida: You're not the man I thought you were.

Augustus: I demand my heart.

Frida: Your fierce wildness has evaporated.

(Augustus snatches Frida's bag.)

Augustus: Give it to me!

Frida: You don't love me. You love love.

Augustus: I love love, very well. You, however, love my disordered affairs because they give you the upper hand in the battle of the sexes for the triumph of the individual ego.

(Augustus opens Frida's bag, gets the package and puts it into his own green bag.)

It belongs to me.

Frida: It is undone. We are haters.

Augustus: Yes, we are enemies.

(Augustus gets up from the table.)

Good night.

(Augustus exits.)

Frida: Good night.

(Frida exits. End of scene.)

Scene Seven. The Hotel Room.

(DAGNY is washing her face at the washstand. STACHU sits on the edge of the bed.)

STACHU: I was dreaming just now before I woke up. Edzin and I were traveling together on an English steamer. We were standing on the top deck, looking out at the beginnings of a huge storm at sea, and suddenly we, Edzin and I, started fighting... flying at one another like cocks, tangling up in a knot, rolling, twisting. He was screaming at me, 'She's mine. She belongs to me.' This man is ridiculous, that's what I was thinking. He is ridiculous. Edzin picked me up, right off my feet, and spun me around and around. I beat his face with my fists. Edzin. What's he to me? So we're friends. What's a friend? Brothers. Ridiculous. He was trying to kill me. He was. He carried me over to the rail to throw me into the sea, and I hit him again and again, but his body was like foam, like the downy loam of the stars, and then, I don't know how, it was a dream after all... I had him in my arms and turned upside-down, and with one big... (Short pause.) I threw Edzin overboard into the sea.

(Pause.)

I have no interest in cause, only in fact. And this is a fact: I am a criminal. I have committed a crime. (Short pause.) I feel as if I am hurrying toward the future. The new will. The superman. The superman who eliminates all those stupid ethical survivals, all those remnants of morality. (Short pause.) I am a completely different man from the man I was three hours ago.

DAGNY: And what shall you be, comrade, three hours from now?

STACHU: Completely insane. (Laughs.) I want to be happy. Happy. (Short pause.) Your hands are so beautiful.

(STACHU kisses DAGNY's hands.)

I have never seen such hands.

DAGNY: Don't. It hurts. (Short pause.) You're hurting me.

STACHU: Love me, love me, love me, mine, mine—

DAGNY: Stop it.

(Pause.)

STACHU: That wasn't very nice of me, was it? All you've been through, of course. (Short pause.) Yes, let's be friends. As you say, comrades and free lovers. Shall we? (Short pause.) Love?

(Pause.)

Say something.

(Pause. A tear rolls down DAGNY's face. End of scene.)

Scene Eight. The Railway Station.

(Wheels. Smoke. A telephone. A railway bench. A spotlight picks up STRINDBERG on the bench.)

STRINDBERG: In Berlin, I am torn away from everything I once knew to be my life. In Berlin, everything is new. Everyone I meet is for the first time. Sometimes they are friendly and… and sometimes…

(The spot fades. Lights up on FRIDA who is on the telephone. She is carelessly dressed for travel and has some luggage.)

FRIDA: Yes, sister, you will be pleased to hear your evil twin is returning to the iron reality. I bend to father's wishes. I leave for Munich immediately. Berlin is a grave. (Short pause.) Alone. One should never show a man that one cares for him. (Short pause.) In my divine idiocy, I expected of the superman— Please, stop laughing. (Short pause.) This I know: August Strindberg is no ordinary animal.

(A steam whistle blows.)

Sister, I have to go. My train— (Short pause.) No, I don't want to hear what the papers— No! I won't listen—

(FRIDA hangs up. The whistle blows. She picks up her luggage. A spotlight picks up STRINDBERG.)

August!

(STRINDBERG turns away.)

August, please, talk to me. Why are you here at the railway station?

STRINDBERG: I am not the one you seek.

FRIDA: You're not well. You're bleeding.

STRINDBERG: In Berlin, I live a thousand deaths.

FRIDA: What's happened to you?

STRINDBERG: Ask the other, the butcher. He knows.

(STRINDBERG breaks away.)

FRIDA: August! Come back—

(STRINDBERG begins to climb to a high place.)

Come back here—

(STRINDBERG climbs. He almost falls.)

August!

(FRIDA runs to where he began to climb.)

Come back. August…

(The spot fades.)

August... August...

(FRIDA attempts to climb. Her skirt is caught. She yanks it free. She comes back down. A whistle blows. EDVARD and AUGUST enter, crossing through the railway station.)

AUGUST: (to EDVARD) Marriage... a rope by which two people hang themselves.

(FRIDA turns to them.)

FRIDA: August?

(AUGUST turns away in a snub. The two men keep walking. FRIDA grabs AUGUST by his sleeve.)

How are you here?

AUGUST: A shortcut to The Pig, if it's any concern of yours.

FRIDA: But...?

AUGUST: Don't get the idea I'm following you. I'm not. Excuse me.

FRIDA: You're not bleeding.

AUGUST: Certainly not.

(A spotlight picks up STRINDBERG high above and climbing dangerously. FRIDA looks at him, and then she looks at AUGUST.)

Excuse me.

(FRIDA begins to climb after STRINDBERG.)

FRIDA: (climbing) August, come back.

EDVARD: Who is she?

AUGUST: A madwoman.

(A steam whistle blows. End of scene.)

Scene Nine. The Black Pig.

(EDVARD and AUGUST are drinking at a table.)

AUGUST: 'You two can go'…?

EDVARD: That's what I said.

AUGUST: And you kissed your bride-to-be auf Wiedersehen?

EDVARD: Stachu was sitting where you are now with his arm around Dagny's body. Her head was so near to him. It seemed so strange to have her eyes, her mouth, her breath so near to him.

AUGUST: I imagine he felt able to talk to his heart's content. That he only needed to hint at a thing, and he was understood.

EDVARD: He laid his head down between her breasts.

AUGUST: She drank in the torrent of his words.

EDVARD: She lowered her head down and bit his neck.

AUGUST: She got all the answers to the many questions she had been wanting to ask a man for such a very long time.

EDVARD: A shudder passed through his body.

AUGUST: A shudder…

EDVARD: Shaking with convulsions as if in extreme pain, clinging to one another, they glided through the door.

(Pause.)

Now, the chain is complete which binds my beginning to my end.

AUGUST: What new nonsense is this, Munch?

EDVARD: Life is an electrical charge consisting of three events: birth, sex, and death.

AUGUST: You're going to kill yourself?

EDVARD: Tonight.

AUGUST: Over a woman? You, Edvard Munch, the man who would marry his bride to the world?

EDVARD: A little while ago, jealousy attacked me with a thousand knives.

AUGUST: (laughs) So you intend to use a knife? Why not a gun? Blow your brains out. Or a strong rope, and hang yourself from one of the lime trees in bloom. Or better yet, bang your head against a wall, tie yourself up with a rope, jump into the river, and hire a passerby to take potshots at your floating corpse with a pistol.

EDVARD: Even before the umbilical cord is cut, we begin to die.

AUGUST: It is ridiculous to kill yourself over a creature with no more worth than a beggar, a peddler of wooden spoons, a bad poet.

EDVARD: No. You're wrong, Strindberg. You're very completely wrong.

AUGUST: About what am I wrong?

EDVARD: Women are people, flesh and blood like you and me.

AUGUST: Man and woman have evolved from two distinct species of monkeys.

EDVARD: I have seen women who were hungry. I have seen them thirsty, in pain, suffering, wanting to live, wanting to die, wanting to love—

(DAGNY enters.)

Love! Dagny, here I am. Here. (Short pause.) I knew you would come back to me. I knew it.

DAGNY: Edzin, please.

EDVARD: My goddess, my muse, never before have you been so beautiful as this very moment.

DAGNY: Enough.

EDVARD: (to AUGUST) I suppose, as a woman-hater, you are unable to see that she is beautiful.

DAGNY: I'm not your property. (To AUGUST.) Who are you?

AUGUST: I am Strindberg.

DAGNY: Never heard of you.

AUGUST: You're hard of hearing? I said, I am Strindberg.

DAGNY: Did you say 'Stind-berg?'

EDVARD: (laughs) 'Stind-berg!'

AUGUST: S, t, r, i, n, d… berg.

DAGNY: 'Stind-berg' in Norwegian means 'big bag of wind.'

EDVARD: He's a writer.

DAGNY: Appropriate.

AUGUST: I am August Adam Samson Caesar Napoleon Edgar Allen Poe Kaiser Nietzsche Strindberg!

(Pause.)

DAGNY: (whispers) Take care, August Strindberg. You are overrated. A rude
    awakening from your dreams of power and greatness lies in store for you.

AUGUST: You lack roundness.

DAGNY: Your coattail is bursting.

AUGUST: Your chief charm here at The Pig lies in being the only available piece
    of feminine furniture.

DAGNY: I compete for my rights. I prefer it.

    (DAGNY opens a small case containing mirrors.)

In fact, I prefer open warfare.

    (AUGUST and DAGNY each select a mirror, and they begin to
    duel, but not before EDVARD scrambles out of the way.)

Wake up, August Strindberg. Awake from your dreams of power.

AUGUST: You pretend to be a spiritual vampire longing for higher things.

DAGNY: I am woman. I pretend nothing.

AUGUST: Learn this, modern woman. The achievement of power is costly.

DAGNY: Costly, yes, and brutal, too. Look what it's done to man.

AUGUST: Aha... inflamed because you're not a man.

DAGNY: No one wants to lower herself.

AUGUST: But man is the stronger.

DAGNY: The stronger beast.

AUGUST: You'll turn the world upside-down.

DAGNY: Only to set it on its feet and follow it to the end.

AUGUST: Bravado!

DAGNY: It is now necessary for man to be improved by woman.

AUGUST: Machismo!

DAGNY: Awake, and rise above your circumstance.

AUGUST: Braggadocio—

(Pause.)

DAGNY: Get up.

AUGUST: How would you improve me?

DAGNY: Perhaps when the ape retreats, the new Buddha appears.

(End of scene.)

Scene Ten. The Industrial Wasteland.

(Smokestacks belching smoke. STRINDBERG enters. He moves here and there. A spotlight tries to follow, but he keeps moving. At last, he is still.)

STRINDBERG: I am August Strindberg.

(FRIDA enters without his knowledge.)

I call upon the unknown powers, the great disorder of the universe. I will myself to fly... to fly in a new element neither air nor water, to fly through eternity dressed in white robes... an airship with wings and sails of purest gossamer...

FRIDA: A one-man flying machine?

STRINDBERG: Who's there?

FRIDA: Only one… one man?

STRINDBERG: Go away.

FRIDA: Alone? By yourself? Without a friend?

STRINDBERG: Stop. Right there. Don't move, or you'll fall.

FRIDA: I'm not going to fall.

STRINDBERG: Stop!

FRIDA: Where will I fall?

STRINDBERG: I see a place, high up, high up in the air, and I see a man fighting, fighting with himself, a terrible battle. Are you an angel or a devil?

FRIDA: Neither. I'm just a friend.

STRINDBERG: I don't know you.

FRIDA: I know you. The whole of Europe bows down before your genius.

STRINDBERG: Europe bows down? Europe?

FRIDA: Yes.

STRINDBERG: Europe is a corpse, a heap of smoldering flags, a calendar of shards, a necklace of ash.

FRIDA: People live as best they can. They're not evil.

STRINDBERG: Nor are they good. (Short pause.) Sons of dust, daughters of dust, in dust they wander.

FRIDA: There's understanding… compassion.

STRINDBERG: The earth is unclean. Life is not good.

FRIDA: Not everyone lives blindly in a world of his own.

STRINDBERG: Shh! (Short pause.) Can you hear?

FRIDA: What?

STRINDBERG: Listen.

(Pause.)

FRIDA: Engines... machines?

STRINDBERG: The cries of the cattle from the slaughterhouse. (Short pause.) There. Did you hear that?

FRIDA: The whistle?

STRINDBERG: Gunshots. (Short pause.) There

(Pause.)

FRIDA: Yes... I can hear it now.

STRINDBERG: The cries?

FRIDA: Yes.

STRINDBERG: Like an ocean of pain between your ears... roaring, rolling, bawling? (Short pause.) When an animal stands in the slaughterhouse, it must put forward its head. Someone taps the animal on its shoulder, and it puts its head forward. Instinctively stretches the neck... forward. Why it doesn't refuse, why it doesn't flinch, doesn't turn, doesn't stampede, nobody will ever know. It stretches, stretches... and then paradise.

FRIDA: Please... you're hurt, you're bleeding, you need a doctor—

STRINDBERG: Stop! You'll fall.

FRIDA: Let me help you.

STRINDBERG: I want to wrap myself in darkness.

(The spot fades. STRINDBERG is gone.)

FRIDA: August—

(FRIDA steps forward. She falls. End of scene.)

Scene Eleven. The Hotel Room.

(AUGUST is asleep in the bed. DAGNY is dancing alone. Finally, AUGUST wakes up.)

AUGUST: Ohh, ohh, ohh…

DAGNY: Well, my toy soldier, how's your little thing this morning? (Laughs.)

AUGUST: (leaping up) Satanskvinnan!

(DAGNY continues to dance.)

I'll have you know I had my penis measured by a team of medical doctors in Stockholm. In the erect posture, it's exactly fourteen centimetres, more than sufficient, they assured me, for a man with a healthy sexual appetite.

DAGNY: Haven't you any sense of humor whatsoever?

AUGUST: Get out of my room.

DAGNY: (laughs) Your room?

AUGUST: Get out of my room this minute, or I'll throw you out with my bare hands.

DAGNY: This is my hotel room, you… bag-of-wind.

AUGUST: Out, out, out… out, I say.

DAGNY: It's my room.

> (DAGNY continues to dance.)

AUGUST: I'll get the superintendent.

> (AUGUST goes to the door and opens it.)

We'll see who's room it is.

> (AUGUST exits, but he trips over STACHU who is sleeping in the doorway.)

Whoa—

STACHU: Good morning, father.

AUGUST: Stachu? What are you doing here?

STACHU: I spent the night sleeping like a dog outside the door in the hope that Dagny—

AUGUST: This is her room?

STACHU: Of course. Who's did you think it was?

AUGUST: Let's get out of here.

STACHU: Now we are enemies, father, and must fight like stags to the death.

AUGUST: Yes, yes, later, Stachu, later. Let's have some breakfast first.

> (AUGUST and STACHU exit. DAGNY dances alone. End of scene.)

Scene Twelve. The Café.

(A table and two chairs. A WAITER serves two plates of food which includes sausages. AUGUST begins eating right away. STACHU doesn't touch his plate. He has a newspaper.)

AUGUST: All the breakfasts I've missed cry out for revenge.

STACHU: Everyone I love is a source of unspeakable suffering and therefore my enemy.

AUGUST: (eating) I have never suffered on account of a woman.

STACHU: That's because you are old and ridiculous, and your organism is very tough. Your sensibilities have yet to reach the evolutionary stage of dependency upon the brain. You are like a hydromedusa which suddenly parts with its sexual organs and sends them off to seek the female. Or, or... (Laughs.) Perhaps you are an amoeba who simply divides. Is that it, Strindberg?

AUGUST: Humph. I am happy. Eat.

STACHU: I don't envy you your happiness. I don't envy the ox his enjoyment of grass. Not even if I'm starving.

AUGUST: Try the sausage.

STACHU: I am suffering because my being is trying to create links with the universe, with the whole of nature. I am suffering because, because I cannot connect, merge, cannot fuse with that creature of bone, tissue, and blood which is my complement, my double: woman. (Short pause.) My phallus is Christ crucified between my legs, nailed to the rotten tree of my body to suffer an eternity. (Laughs.)

AUGUST: Stachu. Eat your breakfast.

STACHU: No. If my belly is full, I won't want to fight. I'll read the paper.

(STACHU reads the paper. Pause.)

AUGUST: Any good gossip?

STACHU: Only that you're going to be married this afternoon.

AUGUST: The Swedish Lion roars!

STACHU: Your father-in-law, the Court Councillor Friedrich Uhl, and his wife, Maria, are arriving in Berlin this morning for the ceremony.

AUGUST: My creditors must be going crazy. Let me show you something.

(AUGUST finds the package in the green bag.)

Stachu, look.

STACHU: A package of meat?

AUGUST: Take it.

STACHU: I told you, I'm not hungry.

AUGUST: Pick it up. Pick it up.

STACHU: If this is an insult, Strindberg, I'll box your ears.

AUGUST: Open it.

STACHU: Open it...?

AUGUST: Go ahead... open it!

(STACHU opens the package.)

STACHU: Ugh... kitchen scraps.

AUGUST: Where's the heart?

STACHU: No heart. Phew... rotten.

AUGUST: Give it back.

STACHU: Gladly… ugh.

AUGUST: I've been robbed, cheated, tricked. (Short pause.) This calls for action.

STACHU: What are you doing?

AUGUST: I'm going home… to bed.

(AUGUST exits.)

STACHU: Come back here, Strindberg. I want to bite your leg.

(End of scene.)

Scene Thirteen. The Industrial Wasteland.

(STRINDBERG is climbing to a high place. A spotlight picks him up. FRIDA climbs after him.)

STRINDBERG: Harpy! Dog!

FRIDA: Are you talking to me?

STRINDBERG: Go away!

FRIDA: Are you talking to me, or to your ex-wife?

STRINDBERG: Dog! Insect!

FRIDA: Are you talking to any woman?

STRINDBERG: I'll push you down.

FRIDA: Out of a thousand women, I'm the one who lacks caution. But I cannot be educated. I'm part of you.

(STRINDBERG reaches the high place. He holds his arms up to the heavens.)

STRINDBERG: I am August Strindberg, and I declare one law, one system, one universe, one element, one formula, one force, one equation, one knowledge, one root, one branch, one fruit, one heaven, one earth, one hell, one, one, one, one, one—

(FRIDA reaches the high place. She grabs STRINDBERG, and they struggle.)

Let go of me—

FRIDA: I'm part of you—

STRINDBERG: Let go—

FRIDA: Your twin, your sister—

STRINDBERG: I will myself to fly—

FRIDA: Your spouse—

STRINDBERG: Fly, fly, fly—

FRIDA: Flesh must tear—

STRINDBERG: Fly—

FRIDA: Souls divide—

(STRINDBERG breaks away. He falls.)

No—

(FRIDA leaps for STRINDBERG, and together, hand-in-hand, they fly.)

STRINDBERG: ⎱
            ⎰ (simultaneous) One, one, one, one, one…
FRIDA:

(End of scene.)

Scene Fourteen. The Bedroom.

(A FIGURE in a masked cowl enters and hides behind a curtain. Pause. AUGUST enters in a rush, looks around here and there. He sits on the bed. The package falls apart in his hands.)

AUGUST: Enter your room alone at night, and someone has beaten you there. You won't see him, but you know he's there. Go to the lunatic asylum… consult the psychiatrist. But they will never cure you. (Short pause.) Where will you go then, all of you who suffer from sleeplessness? Where will you go, insomniacs… all of you who walk the streets in search of the sunrise? What is to be done? Must you humble yourself? Seek God and find the devil?

(Pause.)

I have done penance… as have you. I have mended my ways… as have you. If I put on new heels, the uppers split. Thee is no end to it. If I give up drinking and come home sober, my room is full of demons. If on the other hand I come home drunk, I sleep like an angel. (Short pause.) What is to be done? How should we live our lives?

(AUGUST catches his reflection in a mirror.)

Who… who are you?

(Pause.)

I am the real August Strindberg.

(A spotlight picks up the masked FIGURE moving into view

from behind the curtain. AUGUST has the dagger in his hand.)

Ohh…!

(FRIDA enters.)

FRIDA: I am Frida Uhl, and this is the slaughterhouse. (Short pause.) In the end, we only do two things alone. Once is when we're fearful, and the other is when we die. The rest of consciousness is a community. (Short pause.) Be quick. The chance may not come again.

(AUGUST drops the dagger and goes to the FIGURE. They turn about together, becoming one, and the spot fades. End of scene.)

Scene Fifteen. The Black Pig.

(DAGNY sits at one of the tables, reading a book. EDVARD sits at the other table, drinking. His head is haphazardly wrapped with a great wad of bloody rags for a bandage. STACHU enters.)

STACHU: Edzin!

EDVARD: Oh, it's you. Good evening, good evening.

STACHU: For heaven's sake, what have you done to yourself?

EDVARD: Very glad, indeed. (Short pause.) Sit, sit.

STACHU: Have you been to a doctor?

EDVARD: Well, my dear friend, how are the love operations going today?

STACHU: I don't know what you're talking about.

EDVARD: Straight from the seat of bliss, are we? Dead easy, was it?

STACHU: Edzin, please… what have you done to yourself?

EDVARD: What? This? I broke my head against a wall. What of it? It's nothing to the universe, nothing to the end.

STACHU: You need at least a fresh bandage.

EDVARD: Only a few drops of blood, and… it's good for my art. Look. See? Everyone is looking at me in here, and that gives me an excellent opportunity to jot down a few sketches.

(Picks up a sketch pad.)

Would you like to see? (Short pause.) No?

STACHU: Stop acting like an idiot.

EDVARD: I'm the last generation of a dying race. My life has been full of sickness, longing, death, art. (Short pause.) She… she still loves me.

(Pause.)

STACHU: I… I went home just now to pack my things? And the place was empty, except for a note from my Maschka, my… my mistress? (Laughs.) She's left me for another man. Yes. (Short pause.) I couldn't bear to touch anything in the room. Her impression curved into the bedclothes, the smell of her hair in the pillow. I couldn't do anything but turn the note over again and again, staring at each single letter, examining each fold in the paper touched by her fingers.

(Pause.)

EDVARD: You idiot.

(End of scene.)

Scene Sixteen. The Island of Heligoland.

> (AUGUST and FRIDA are walking on a high cliff overlooking the sea. FRIDA wears pajamas with a fig leaf and a wedding veil. AUGUST wears pajamas with a fig leaf and a top hat.)

AUGUST: Well, and here we are on the island of Heligoland… walking on the cliffs, looking down upon the sea.

FRIDA: Six days we've been here, waiting for your divorce papers.

AUGUST: Don't you trust me?

FRIDA: I believe in your honesty, but…

AUGUST: You believe but…? But what?

FRIDA: My sister.

AUGUST: Oh, of course, your sister. She has a problem?

FRIDA: She doesn't know you, August. Not like I do. (Short pause.) After all, your assurances to her that your papers were in order have proved to be incorrect.

AUGUST: She's right, but it's not my fault.

FRIDA: Mitzi is returning to Vienna tomorrow, and I must go with her.

AUGUST: What? We're to be divorced before we're married?

FRIDA: No, not that. Let's jump into the sea.

AUGUST: Good idea. Why prolong the inevitable?

> (They take a step forward. Pause.)

FRIDA: Do you think it's cold?

AUGUST: What will your parents say?

FRIDA: I don't want to talk about them.

(They take a step forward. Pause.)

AUGUST: Men of honor need no written agreements.

FRIDA: When you and I are together only one man of honor is present.

AUGUST: How am I to interpret that?

FRIDA: Anyway you please.

(FRIDA bolts for the edge of the cliff. AUGUST pulls her back in the nick of time.)

AUGUST: Come here.

(They kiss. End of scene.)

(End of play.)

Printed in Canada

AGMV MARQUIS
IMPRIMEUR INC.
Membre du Groupe Scabrini